DO YOU YOU KNOW

WHAT'S HAPPENING IN YOUR STATE?

Asrar Johnson

Studio Noir

PUBLISHING

What every beauty professional needs to know about state regulations and industry advocacy.

Book cover design and interior layout provided by Self Publish Me Publishing Consulting and Book Design Services for Independent Authors. Selfpublishme.com | email: info@selfpublishme.com

To my dad—who taught me to pay attention, to stand tall in the storm and to never be silent when it matters most.

I love you!

Table of Contents

Foreword   7

Introduction   9

Chapter 1 Wake Up, Beautiful People   11

Chapter 2 Know the Board That Knows You   14

Chapter 3 When the Floor Falls Out   19

Chapter 4 Understanding the Process – How Laws Are Made and Why They Matter to You   24

Chapter 5 Reading Between the Lines – How to Track and Understand Legislation   29

Chapter 6 Connecting with Your Industry Community   35

Chapter 7 When the Public Doesn't Understand Our Value   38

Chapter 8 Building Unity Within the Industry   41

Chapter 9 Advocacy Beyond the Chair — How to Stay Engaged Year-Round   44

Chapter 10 The Power of Professional Unity   47

Chapter 11 Do You Know What's Happening in Your State?   50

Chapter 12 Building a Culture of Ongoing Engagement   55

Chapter 13 Where Do We Go from Here?   58

Acknowledgments   65

Appendix A Understanding the Legislative Process & Session
Timelines   66

Appendix B Advocacy, Professional, and Legislative Resources 69

Appendix C Templates & Scripts   71

Appendix D Additional Resources   80

Appendix E Professional Development & Leadership Pathways in the
Beauty and Barbering Industry   83

Appendix F Glossary of Terms   86

Appendix G Continuing Your Advocacy Journey   89

Appendix H Sample Advocacy Journal Pages   92

Notes & Reflections   94

Author's Note   96

Foreword

As the Lead Organizer of The Concerned Beauty and Barber Professionals (TheCBBP) and the Lead Advocate of Politics Beauty and Barber (PBB), it is hard to find beauty and barber professionals who are dedicated to protecting the integrity of the beauty and barber industry. Asrar Johnson is one of those rare professionals. Asrar's commitment to upholding high standards in the industry, her tenacity in advocating to protect the professional license in Oklahoma and her passion for the profession has garnered her insights that are beneficial to beauty and barber professionals everywhere.

—Tamara Johnson-Shealey

Introduction

"The Industry is changing-but are we paying attention?"

There is a storm quietly brewing in the beauty industry-one that many licensed professionals don't see coming until it's too late. We are artists, caregivers, confidence-builders, and community leaders. But beyond the salon chairs and barber stations, there's another world that impacts us deeply: the world of politics, policy, and state regulation.

I never imagined I'd be writing a book like this. I'm, a Master Dermotricologist, certified Trichologist, licensed cosmetologist and cosmetology instructor, as well as a business owner. I spend my days helping people with hair, scalp and skin disorders, encouraging my clients and colleagues, and building a better future for our profession. But when Oklahoma House Bill 1030 (HB1030) came across my radar, it shook me.

HB1030 was. More than just a piece of legislation-it represented a potential shift in how our entire profession is governed. The bill proposed to extend the existence of the Oklahoma State Board of Cosmetology and Barbering. Without it, our governing agency would be left without clear support or direction. The Governor vetoed the bill. And now, we are standing at a crossroads, unsure of what happens next.

Many professionals I spoke with had no idea what the bill even was. Some were frustrated but unaware. Others were indifferent or too discouraged to care. And some said, "I wish I had known sooner." That broke my heart. Because in an industry that's rooted in human connection, wellness, transformation, we can't afford to be disconnected from the decisions being made about us-without us.

This book is a resource, a guide, and a call to action. It's not just about HB1030. It's about what happens when we don't know who governs our licenses, what bills are being passed, or what regulations are being debated behind closed doors. It's about waking up and staying woke-not in the trendy sense, but in the practical, professional sense.

Whether you're a new graduate, a seasoned educator, an independent stylist, a barber, or someone running a multi-chair salon, you need to know what's happening in your state. Because ignorance is not just risky-it's dangerous to your career, your livelihood, and the legacy of our industry.

We cannot protect what we are unaware of. And we cannot lead what we do not understand.

Let this book be your compass. Use it to understand the systems that govern your license. Share it with your peers. Teach from it. Talk about it. Build action from it. Because if we don't, we risk becoming the last generation that had a real say in what it means to be a licensed professional in cosmetology and barbering.

Let's begin.

Chapter 1
Wake Up, Beautiful People

Why Every Licensed Professional Needs to Pay Attention Now

You can be one of the best stylists, barbers, estheticians, or educators in the industry—but if you don't know what's happening behind the scenes of your state's legislation, then you're standing on shaky ground. Too many of us are focused solely on what's happening behind the chair or at the treatment table, and we're missing what's happening under the Capitol dome.

We live in a world where regulations can change with the stroke of a pen. And yet, in our industry, it's not uncommon to hear people say:

- "I didn't know that was even on the table."

- "That doesn't affect me—I just do nails."

- "I'll worry about it when something happens."

But by the time "something happens," it's often too late.

The Danger of Being Disconnected

In 2025, House Bill 1030 was introduced in Oklahoma to extend the authority of the Oklahoma State Board of Cosmetology and Barbering. It seemed like a simple extension—a necessary one. After all, this board doesn't just hand out licenses. It protects consumers, sets

standards, ensures safety, and gives our profession structure.
But the governor vetoed the bill.

And that veto didn't just put a pin in the process—it potentially destabilized the very agency that oversees five distinct but interconnected professions: **cosmetology, barbering, nail technology, aesthetics, and massage therapy.** Without action or adjusted language in the law, we are left without a strong jurisdiction to move under. And without that, our licenses, our standards, our professional identity could be on the line.

Now, let's be clear: this isn't just about Oklahoma.

Across the country, states are re-evaluating licensing boards, consolidating them, or in some cases, attempting to dissolve them altogether in the name of "deregulation" or "streamlining." The beauty and wellness industries are being grouped under broad occupational umbrellas with little understanding of our unique needs and public health implications.

When that happens, the consequences can be devastating:

- **Lower standards for education and safety**

- **Increased consumer harm**

- **Professionals losing their ability to earn a living**

And yet, many in our industry don't even know these conversations are happening.
Why Our Silence Is a Problem
The industry has talent. We have power. We have presence. But we are not showing up where it counts most—in legislative and policy spaces.
There's no excuse for staying uninformed when your license—your livelihood—is at risk. You may not be a politician or a lobbyist, but you

are a professional with a voice. That voice should not only speak over blow dryers and at shampoo bowls—it should be heard in Capitol buildings, at city council meetings, in school board sessions, and on public forums.

This isn't about politics in the party sense. This is about professional politics—the decisions that dictate whether your license exists next year or if your curriculum is gutted or if your board is replaced by an umbrella agency with no beauty or wellness expertise.

From Passive to Powerful

We have a decision to make. We can either keep our heads down and pretend none of this matters—or we can lift our heads up, get informed, and get involved.

Being a professional isn't just about technique and talent. It's about advocacy. It's about knowing who's making the decisions that affect your practice—and holding them accountable.

This chapter is your warning shot. The rest of this book is your guide. Let's wake up, show up, and speak up—before the next bill goes through unnoticed.

Action Step: Self-Assessment
- **Do you know who governs your license in your state?**

- **Do you know how to find proposed legislation that affects your industry?**

- **When was the last time you contacted your state board, local legislator, or attended an industry-related hearing?**

If you're unsure or answered "no," don't beat yourself up. But let this be the moment you start changing that.

Chapter 2

Know the Board That Knows You

Understanding the Role and Reach of Your
State Regulatory Agency

Let's be honest—when most people think about their state board, they don't exactly light up with excitement. In fact, "the board" can seem like this distant, rule-setting authority we only hear about when someone gets fined or a school gets audited. But your state board is far more than a name on your license renewal. It is the foundation that makes your career possible—and protects your ability to earn, grow, and serve. If it disappears or weakens, your professional identity is at risk.

So let's break it down.

What Does a State Board Actually Do?

Your state board is not just there to regulate. It's there to:

- **Define the scope of your profession**
  (What you are legally allowed to do.)

- **Approve schools and curriculums**
  (What is taught, how long, and by whom.)

- **Issue and renew licenses**
  (And enforce continuing education requirements, if any.)

- **Investigate consumer complaints and enforce sanitation rules**
  (This is a public safety issue—not just a beauty standard.)

- **Hold hearings, assess fines, and suspend or revoke licenses when needed**
  (Accountability protects the profession.)

In Oklahoma, the State Board of Cosmetology and Barbering covers cosmetologists, barbers, nail technicians, aestheticians, and massage therapists. That's a wide reach—especially compared to other states where these services fall under separate boards or umbrella licensing systems.

Why It Matters Who Governs You

Imagine waking up one day and learning your board has been absorbed into a general occupational licensing agency—with no professionals from your field on the board. Or worse: that your license requirements have been slashed to near-nothing, putting you on the same playing field as someone with no formal education or clinical experience.

This is what's happening in several states right now. And it often starts quietly, under the radar, through legislative bills that sound "harmless" or "streamlining." But those bills have the power to:

- Eliminate licensing altogether

- Shift control to people outside our industry

- Undercut education and training standards

- Create confusion across schools, salons, and spas

When HB1030 was vetoed, it didn't just block a bill—it signaled the beginning of uncertainty. If we don't have a board—or we don't know where we're moving—then everything tied to that agency becomes vulnerable.

Who Sits at the Table (And Why You Should Care)

State boards usually include a mix of:

- Licensed professionals (cosmetologists, barbers, educators)

- Public members (representing consumer interests)

- Sometimes school owners, instructors, or even medical professionals

These people are often appointed by the governor or another state official. Their decisions are made in open meetings—but very few industry professionals show up to those meetings. Fewer still submit public comments or provide input.

That's where the disconnect starts: **we don't show up, so we don't get heard.** But when you know who is sitting at the table—and how to access them—you can:

- Advocate for changes that help your profession

- Challenge proposals that hurt schools, students, or professionals

- Stay ahead of decisions that directly affect your license

Building a Relationship with Your Board

Here's the truth: your board doesn't have to be scary, distant, or difficult. You can—and should—build a relationship with them.

Start by:

- Visiting the board's website regularly

- Signing up for newsletters or email updates

- Attending public meetings (in person or virtually)

- Asking questions about changes or pending rules

- Letting them know you're invested in the future of the profession

When professionals show up respectfully and consistently, boards listen. But when we're silent, decisions get made without us.

Quick Reference: Key Functions of a State Board

Function	Why It Matters
Licensing	Legitimizes your ability to work
Education Approval	Ensures quality of training
Rule Enforcement	Maintains public health and safety
Continuing Education	Encourages career growth and competency
Complaint Resolution	Protects both professionals and consumers

Action Step: Know Your Board

- Who is on your state board right now?

- When is their next public meeting?

- How can you attend, comment, or ask a question?

You are not *just a stylist,* a *barber,* or *technician.* You are a licensed professional. And that license is only as strong as the structure that upholds it.

Chapter 3
When the Floor Falls Out

The Real-World Consequences of Deregulation in Cosmetology and Barbering

It often starts with a single sentence in a bill:

"This measure eliminates the requirement for a state license to perform cosmetic services."

One sentence that has the power to erase years of professional training, eliminate protections for consumers, and flood the market with unqualified service providers—all in the name of "cutting red tape."

In this chapter, we're diving into **real consequences** of deregulation, with examples that show how fast things can unravel when a profession loses its seat at the table.

What Is Deregulation—and Why Does It Sound So Good to Lawmakers?

Deregulation is the process of removing or reducing state oversight in an industry.

On paper, it's often pitched as a win for:

- Free enterprise

- Easier business startups

- Less government spending

- "Reducing barriers to entry"

But what many lawmakers—and the public—don't always understand is that **our "barriers" are not random.**

They are built to:

- Protect the health and safety of the public

- Ensure professional competence

- Uphold the value of licensed education and training

When those barriers are stripped away, we're not looking at "freedom." We're looking at chaos.

Case Studies: When Licenses Are Weakened or Wiped Out

Utah (2012–2020): Deregulation by Division

In Utah, lawmakers began rolling back requirements for certain services, including hair braiding, makeup artistry, and even some nail services. At first, it seemed harmless—why license people who weren't working with chemicals?

But the gradual peeling back of licensure led to:

- Widespread confusion about who could legally offer what

- A flooded marketplace with untrained practitioners

- Less respect for licensed professionals who had gone through 1,600+ hours of training

Educators reported a drop in enrollment as prospective students chose cheaper, faster, and now "unregulated" routes. Established professionals faced price undercutting and client safety concerns.

Indiana (2018): The Push to Eliminate Licensing Entirely

Indiana proposed eliminating licenses for cosmetologists and barbers altogether. After massive pushback—including viral social media campaigns and professionals showing up at the capitol—the bill was eventually dropped.

But it showed us just how close a total wipeout can come.
Many professionals in the state didn't hear about the bill until it was nearly too late.

Texas (2019): Barber and Cosmetology Boards Merged

In Texas, lawmakers combined the barber and cosmetology boards, claiming it would streamline operations. What followed was years of confusion:

- License delays

- Instructor and school oversight gaps

- Thousands of professionals unsure of how their scope of practice had changed

While not a full deregulation, the merger created widespread confusion among schools and professionals, leading to the loss of many businesses due to paperwork complications and the spread of misinformation.

Why It Matters for Oklahoma

If HB1030 had passed, it would've **extended the timeline for the existing board to remain in place**. But with the veto, we are now in a dangerous limbo—**no agency is clearly identified to take over**, and there's no timeline or transition plan.

That uncertainty opens the door for:

- Fragmentation of services (splitting licenses between different departments)

- Loss of representation on advisory boards

- Education cuts or consolidation

- A breakdown in how complaints, inspections, and renewals are handled

And if we're not careful? Full deregulation isn't a fantasy—it's a very real possibility.

When Regulation Leaves, So Do Standards

Without licensing:

- Schools suffer (less enrollment, more closures)

- Prices drop—but so does service quality

- Clients get hurt or harmed, and there's no accountability

- Your professional identity is weakened

You didn't train for months or years just to compete with someone who took a weekend course on YouTube.

Action Step: Share the Stories

Start conversations in your salon or classroom using the case studies from this chapter. Ask:

- "What would happen to your job if licenses were eliminated?"

- "Do you think your clients know what we're facing?"

- "How can we speak up before we lose more ground?"

Your voice has power—but only if it's used.

Chapter 4

Understanding the Process – How Laws Are Made and Why They Matter to You

Many professionals in the beauty and wellness industry have built their careers on talent, skill, and service—but very few are taught how to follow the laws that govern the very licenses they hold. Legislative processes may seem far removed from our day-to-day work behind the chair or in the treatment room, but in truth, they have the power to change our entire livelihood with the stroke of a pen.

So let's break it down. Understanding the legislative process is not just a matter of civic education—it's now a professional survival skill.

1. Where It All Starts: A Bill Is Born

Every law begins as a **bill**—a proposal for a new law or a change to an existing one. In Oklahoma (and in most states), a bill can be introduced by a **state senator or representative**. The person who introduces the bill is called the **author**.

Sometimes the idea for a bill comes from a politician. But more often, it's born from pressure by:

- Lobbyists

- Industry groups

- Concerned citizens

- Regulatory agencies

- Political agendas

In our case, the bill that affects our governing agency (HB1030) didn't come out of nowhere. It was born from conversations—many of which happened without the input or awareness of the professionals it affects.

2. Committees: The Gatekeepers

Once a bill is introduced, it doesn't go straight to a vote. First, it's assigned to a **committee**—a small group of legislators who specialize in that topic.

The committee stage is *crucial* because:

- They hold the power to move the bill forward or stop it entirely

- Amendments (changes) to the bill can be made here

- Public hearings may be held—but not always

- This is often where bills are quietly killed or rewritten

If the committee votes to move it forward, it goes to the **full House or Senate** for debate and a vote.

3. Debate, Amendments, and Voting

In the House or Senate chamber:

- Lawmakers **debate** the bill

- **Amendments** can still be added

- A final vote is taken

If the bill passes in one chamber, it must go through **the same process again** in the other (House or Senate, depending on where it started).

Only after both chambers agree on the exact same version does the bill move on to the **Governor's desk**.

4. The Governor's Role

The Governor can:

- **Sign the bill** into law

- **Veto the bill**, rejecting it

- Do nothing, which sometimes still allows the bill to become law, depending on the timing

In the case of **HB1030**, the Governor chose to **veto** the bill. This means that the agency reorganization effort was rejected—at least for now.

But the story doesn't stop there...

5. What Happens After a Veto?

A veto is not always the end. Legislators can attempt an **override**, which typically requires a **supermajority vote**—usually two-thirds of both the House and the Senate.

Overrides are rare but powerful.

Alternatively, lawmakers can **reintroduce the bill** in a future session, possibly with **new language** to address objections or concerns.

This is the phase we are in now: watching, waiting, and urging those in power to adjust the bill to support—not dissolve—our agency.

6. Why You *Must* Pay Attention

If you're thinking, *"This seems complicated—I just want to do hair, nails, or skincare,"* you're not alone.

But here's the truth:

You can't afford not to care.

When you don't track what's happening at the state level:

- You won't know when your profession is being dismantled until it's too late.

- You miss your chance to write, call, or show up before decisions are made.

- You leave your license in the hands of people who have never worked in your shoes.

7. Becoming an Industry Advocate

You don't need a law degree to be effective. You just need to:

- Learn the process

- Know who your legislators are

- Speak up when it counts

Every professional should be familiar with:

- The Oklahoma State Legislature website

- Bill tracking tools (we'll go into more detail in the next chapter)

- Contact information for your representative and senator

When thousands of voices rise together, we *can* influence what happens in the Capitol.

Closing Thoughts: Your Power Is in Your Participation

Laws don't get passed by accident. And they don't get vetoed by chance.

This chapter isn't just a civic lesson—it's a reminder that *your license is tied to policy*.
Every lawmaker who votes on your future is elected to represent *you*.

So if we want to protect our professions, preserve our agency, and move forward with dignity and power, we must not only **understand** the process—but become a part of it.

Chapter 5

Reading Between the Lines – How to Track and Understand Legislation

You've likely heard someone say, "They passed a bill," or "It's going to committee," but how many of us actually know how to *find*, *read*, or *track* these bills ourselves?

In today's climate—especially with what's happening in Oklahoma—we can no longer afford to just wait on someone else to interpret policy for us. **We need to know how to navigate the legislative process ourselves.**

This chapter is your guide.

1. Why Tracking Bills Matters

When a new piece of legislation is proposed, it doesn't just impact the people in the room where it's written—it can change the lives of thousands of professionals like you and me.

Tracking bills helps you:

- Stay aware of what's being proposed

- Catch damaging language early

- Prepare your business or career for changes

- Alert others in the industry who might be unaware

- Know when and how to act—before it's too late

2. Where to Start: Oklahoma Legislature Website

Every state has a legislative website where citizens can look up laws, bills, and actions taken. In Oklahoma, that site is: **Oklegislature.gov**

This is the *official* hub to:

- Search current and past bills

- Read bill summaries

- Track progress

- See voting records

- Contact authors or committee members

You don't need a login. You just need time and willingness to look.

3. Understanding the Anatomy of a Bill

When you click on a bill (like **HB1030**), you'll see several key components:

a. Bill Number – The official ID, such as "HB1030" (House Bill 1030).

b. Title – A brief summary of what the bill is about. It may say something like "An Act relating to professions and occupations; abolishing the State Board of Cosmetology and Barbering."

c. Authors – The lawmakers who sponsored or co-authored the bill.

d. Status – Shows where the bill is in the process: introduced, in committee, passed, vetoed, etc.

e. Full Text – This is the body of the bill. It includes proposed changes to the law. Some parts may be struck through (old) and others underlined (new).

f. Actions Taken – Every step the bill has taken: who voted, what happened in committee, when it was read, etc.

g. Fiscal Impact Reports – These show how much implementing the bill could cost or save the state.

h. Amendments – These are edits made after the bill is filed. They can be minor—or completely change the meaning of a bill.

4. Tips for Reading Legal Language

Let's be honest: Legal language can feel like reading a foreign language.

Here's how to make it easier:

a. Focus on keywords – Words like *abolish*, *repeal*, *transfer*, *remove*, and *amend* carry serious weight.

b. Use the strikethroughs and underlines – Bills often show what's being removed or added.

c. Read summaries first – Many bills come with a brief explanation at the top. Start there.

d. Don't read it all at once – Focus on the parts that mention your agency or profession.

e. Ask for help – Contact your legislator's office or an industry advocate for clarification.

5. Setting Alerts and Tracking Progress

You don't have to manually check the legislature's website every day. There are tools to help:

Oklahoma Legislature Bill Tracker
You can create a free account on the oklegislature.gov website and:

- Follow specific bills

- Get email notifications when a bill moves or changes

- Download PDFs to share with colleagues

LegiScan.com
A user-friendly site that allows you to search by state and issue.

Capitol Watchdogs (Industry Groups)
Stay connected to local or national beauty industry watchdogs or coalitions. They often send alerts when urgent legislation appears.

6. Becoming a Trusted Source in Your Circle

Once you learn how to track bills, **don't keep it to yourself**.

Become that person in your salon, school, or suite who says:

- "Here's the bill number, read it."

- "It's going to a vote on Monday."

- "Contact your legislator here."

This builds credibility and unity. It helps transform confusion into clarity—and passivity into power.

7. Real-World Example: Tracking HB1030

Let's walk through the steps you would've taken to track **HB1030**:

1. Go to oklegislature.gov

2. Click **"Legislation"** > **"Basic Bill Search"**

3. Type in "HB1030" and hit search

4. Read the **bill title and full text**

5. Scroll to **"Actions Taken"** to see movement

6. Look for **committees assigned**, **votes**, and **amendments**

7. If signed or vetoed, check the Governor's decisions

Knowing how to do this will allow you to follow *any* future bill that threatens or supports your profession.

Final Thoughts: If You Can Read Hair Color Formulas, You Can Read Legislation

It might seem intimidating now—but remember this:

If you've mastered color theory, product chemistry, state board exams, or client consultations—then you already have the mental power to understand legislative language.

What we need now is a shift in mindset: from depending on others to becoming educated professionals who know exactly what's going on at the state level.

Because this isn't just politics.
It's **your livelihood**.

Chapter 6

Connecting with Your Industry Community

I n a time when legislation and regulatory changes threaten the very structure of our professional licenses, community becomes more than a buzzword — it becomes a necessity. This chapter is dedicated to understanding the power of industry connection, especially when policies, politics, and public perception are shifting rapidly.

Why We Must Stay Connected

One of the reasons misinformation and apathy spread so quickly in cosmetology and barbering is because too many professionals operate in silos. Many work independently or within small teams, and few are part of larger professional associations, unions, or policy groups. Without intentional connection, it becomes easy to miss crucial developments — until it's too late.

As seen in Oklahoma's HB1030 situation, **a lack of unified industry voice made it easier for the bill to move forward unchecked**, with many professionals unaware of what was at stake. Imagine if thousands had spoken up earlier — the story might have played out differently.

Types of Industry Connections That Matter

1. Professional Associations:

Organizations like the Professional Beauty Association (PBA), the National Interstate Council of State Boards of Cosmetology (NIC), and **The Concerned Beauty and Barber Professionals (CBBP)** serve as watchdogs and communication hubs. CBBP, in particular, has been instrumental in raising awareness about policy changes affecting the beauty and barbering industries. Their work includes legislative alerts, industry mobilization, and community engagement. You can learn more about their initiatives or get involved at *www.thecbbp.org.*

If you're not a member of any professional organization, now is the time to consider joining. These groups often provide vital updates, represent our interests in legislative spaces, and offer resources for staying informed and empowered.

2. Online Communities & Forums:
While social media has its distractions, Facebook groups, Reddit threads, and LinkedIn forums tailored to beauty professionals often alert members to legislative changes, licensing shifts, and educational events.

3. State Board Meetings & Public Forums:
Whether attending in person or online, showing up at meetings (especially those posted on your state board's calendar) is essential. It's where proposals are introduced, where you can hear public concerns, and where your voice can be part of the public record.

4. Networking Events & Expos:
Events like hair shows, educator symposiums, and continuing education classes aren't just about techniques. They're an opportunity to hear from peers in other parts of the state — or the country — and compare what's happening in your area with theirs.

Building Your Own Micro-Community
If you don't see the kind of connection you need, **create it**. Start a group chat, email chain, or monthly meetup with other professionals you trust. This can be as informal as texting updates about board meetings or as organized as forming a watch group for legislation.

Having a small, informed tribe of like-minded professionals can spark big change. You don't have to lead a movement alone, but you can *help ignite one* by simply staying informed and inviting others to do the same.

"When We Show Up, We Are Counted"

Policy-makers, state boards, and government agencies don't typically take notice of individuals until those individuals become a collective. Showing up in numbers—through petitions, emails, or physical presence—is how we protect our industry from being misunderstood or dismantled.

This chapter isn't just about connection for the sake of networking. It's about preparing your industry for advocacy, unity, and long-term sustainability. Our licenses, our professions, and our futures depend on it.

Chapter 7
When the Public Doesn't Understand
Our Value

One of the most unsettling truths professionals in cosmetology and barbering must confront is this: **the general public often does not fully understand what we do, why it matters, or how we are trained and regulated.** And in times of legislative threat, that lack of understanding becomes dangerous.

The Misconception: "It's Just Hair"

Far too often, policymakers and the public dismiss our industry as something casual or purely cosmetic. They reduce our skill set to just "doing hair," not realizing that we are trained in sanitation, skin integrity, chemical application, anatomy, safety protocols, and even client wellness. This oversimplification is a major reason why deregulation bills can gain traction—people simply don't know better.

They don't realize that poor technique can cause burns, infections, or hair loss. They don't see the risk of untrained hands handling chemical peels, microneedling, or massage therapy without understanding contraindications. **Licensing isn't just a gatekeeping tool; it's public protection.**

The Consequences of Being Undervalued

When the public doesn't value your profession:

- It becomes easier for lawmakers to justify cutting regulation.

- It becomes harder to secure funding for schools, training programs, and continuing education.

- It becomes more likely that misinformation will spread unchecked.

- It contributes to low industry morale and burnout, especially when professionals feel disrespected or unseen.

Part of the Blame: Our Industry's Silence

It's not entirely the public's fault—**our industry has not always done a great job educating people about our training, licensing, and expertise.** Many clients have never seen the back of a license or heard about state board requirements. When was the last time you told a client about your continuing education or sanitation protocols?

We have grown comfortable operating behind the scenes, creating beauty, confidence, and wellness — but not always speaking out about the depth and breadth of our professional knowledge.

What We Can Do

1. Educate One Client at a Time:
Start small. Share snippets with your clients about your certifications, training hours, and the science behind what you do. For example: "When I took my licensing exam, I had to know how to prevent chemical burns and bloodborne pathogen transmission."

2. Promote Your License Visibly:
Make sure your current license is displayed and easy to read. It's not just a legal requirement—it's a subtle way to show professionalism and credibility.

3. Participate in Public Awareness Campaigns:
Whether it's through your professional associations or your own social media, talk about why regulation matters. Highlight the *why* behind your craft.

4. Encourage Industry-Wide Media Involvement:
The media won't tell our story unless we give it to them. Writing op-eds, blog posts, or participating in industry podcasts and interviews helps shift public perception.

How This Applies to Legislation Like HB1030

When Oklahoma's HB1030 appeared, many outside the industry had no reason to question it. They didn't realize the difference between a licensed professional and an unregulated one. They didn't know how vulnerable clients could be in a deregulated market. And they didn't recognize the economic engine this industry fuels in both urban and rural communities.

Legislation that seeks to diminish our industry often thrives on silence and ignorance. But once people understand our role—not just as stylists or barbers, but as health-conscious, skilled professionals — they begin to care.

Chapter 8
Building Unity Within the Industry

When faced with political uncertainty or the threat of deregulation, our strength lies in numbers—but only if those numbers are united. One of the challenges we face in cosmetology, barbering, aesthetics, nail technology, and massage therapy is fragmentation. While our professions share similar roots in wellness, care, and technical skill, we often operate in silos. That has to change.

The Current Divide

There are several divisions in our industry that weaken our collective power:

- **Generational divides** — Younger professionals may not understand the battles older professionals fought to secure standards and protections.

- **Modality divides** — Barbers may not relate to aestheticians, massage therapists may not identify with cosmetologists, and nail techs may feel overlooked entirely.

- **Salon vs. Suite vs. Solo** — The rise of independent suite ownership has empowered many but also created distance

41

from traditional salon structures, where camaraderie and shared learning used to thrive.

- **Licensed vs. Unlicensed spaces** — With deregulation and social media platforms, more people operate in gray areas. Some professionals are working without licenses, unknowingly or otherwise, undermining the legitimacy of the industry as a whole.

Why Unity Is Essential

Legislators don't see all these nuanced differences—they see one *industry*. And when that industry is disjointed or silent, it becomes easy to ignore or dismiss. But when we stand together:

- Our voices are louder and more credible.

- We can lobby more effectively.

- We can share resources across specialties.

- We can protect not only our licenses but our livelihoods.

Strategies for Building Industry Unity

1. Cross-Disciplinary Collaboration:
Attend and support events outside your immediate specialty. If you're a cosmetologist, attend barber or massage therapy town halls. If you're a nail tech, partner with an esthetician on community wellness events.

2. Industry Forums and Online Communities:
Use platforms like Facebook groups, Clubhouse rooms, or even TikTok trends to connect with others in beauty and wellness. Unity can be sparked by something as simple as a shared hashtag or dialogue.

3. Mentorship and Inter-Generational Knowledge Sharing:
Older professionals can offer historical perspective; younger ones often bring new tech and trends. Instead of judging each other, we should be learning from one another.

4. Joint Advocacy Efforts:
When fighting a bill like HB1030, align with professionals across all sectors. Co-author letters, host joint meetings, and sign group petitions. Let lawmakers see we're not just "hair people" or "massage people"—we are **professionals across sectors** united for public safety, economic growth, and wellness.

5. Stop Competing and Start Cooperating:
We are not each other's competition. Unlicensed, unregulated practitioners and legislation that threatens our standards are the competition. As long as we keep battling each other over prices, trends, or aesthetics, we stay distracted from the bigger issues.

Unity as a Legacy

If we can create a more united front in the face of deregulation and legislative attacks, we won't just save our licenses — we'll elevate the industry for the next generation. We'll leave a legacy of advocacy, awareness, and mutual support. That's the kind of impact that lasts far longer than a trend or treatment.

Chapter 9
Advocacy Beyond the Chair — How to Stay Engaged Year-Round

A dvocacy isn't a seasonal event. It doesn't begin and end with a bill. The fight to protect and elevate our professions must become a way of life—woven into our conversations, our business practices, and our community presence. Whether you're behind the chair, at the front desk, in a suite, or managing a team, there are ongoing ways to stay involved.

Why Year-Round Advocacy Matters

Legislation doesn't always happen in public view. Often, discussions and drafts occur in quiet committee rooms, over phone calls, or at closed-door meetings long before the public hears about it. By the time most professionals catch wind of it, it's almost too late. Ongoing engagement helps us stay informed before decisions are made **about us—without us.**

Ways to Stay Informed and Active

1. Subscribe to Legislative Trackers and Alerts
There are platforms such as LegiScan, TrackBill, and your state legislature's website where you can follow bills by topic, keyword, or agency. Some associations even offer curated alerts.

2. Build Relationships with Legislators

Identify your state representative and senator. Write to them, introduce yourself, and invite them to your business. Help them understand what your profession involves and how regulation impacts public health and the economy. The goal is to become a **trusted voice** before a crisis hits.

3. Join or Form Local Advocacy Groups

Whether it's a group chat, a Facebook group, or an in-person roundtable, connect with like-minded professionals in your region. Make a habit of reviewing news together, contacting lawmakers, and showing up to Capitol events as a collective.

4. Attend Public Meetings

Even when the issue isn't directly about cosmetology or barbering, show up. You'll gain insight into how your state government operates, and when something *does* arise, you'll already be a familiar face in the room.

5. Host Advocacy Days in Your Business

Dedicate one day a quarter to "legislative awareness." Place flyers in your business, talk to clients about pending bills, and encourage other professionals to take action. Advocacy doesn't need to be boring—it can be branded, stylish, and powerful.

6. Use Social Media Strategically

Share updates on what's happening, tag officials, and offer education—not just outrage. Use your influence to inform others with clarity and professionalism. A well-worded Instagram post can move mountains when shared across the industry.

7. Support Political Action Committees (PACs)

Organizations that form PACs help fund advocacy efforts, sponsor legislation, or block harmful proposals. Your donation may feel small, but combined with others, it becomes a real force.

Balancing Advocacy with Everyday Business

Being politically active doesn't mean neglecting your business—it can actually **enhance it**. Clients trust professionals who are informed and proactive. You're also protecting your investment. Whether you've spent $5,000 or $50,000 on your education, license, and tools, you deserve a system that respects that.

It's not about becoming political—it's about being professional in a political world.

Chapter 10
The Power of Professional Unity

In times of uncertainty, change, or disruption—like what we're experiencing now in Oklahoma—one truth becomes glaringly clear: **we are stronger together**.

This chapter is about more than collaboration. It's about **intentional unity** in the beauty and barbering industry. It's about going beyond social media rants and group chat frustrations and moving into collective power, influence, and resilience.

The Disjointed Landscape

Despite how interconnected we seem thanks to social platforms, our industry remains deeply **fragmented**. Barbers in one corner. Estheticians in another. Nail techs over here. Cosmetologists over there. Massage therapists in a completely different circle. Each group often fights its own battles in silos, and because of that, we lack a unified voice.

That division weakens our influence. Legislators don't hear one strong, clear message—they hear noise, or worse, nothing at all.

Why Unity Matters Now More Than Ever

Let's reflect on the current legislative threat: the potential deregulation of our governing agency in Oklahoma. This isn't just a bill affecting paperwork. This is an unraveling of standards, protections, and respect for our trades.

Without a **collective response**, the narrative gets shaped without us. When we don't show up, others decide our fate.

But when we stand **together**, we shift the conversation. We show strength. We educate. We influence policy. We protect the legacy and integrity of our professions for future generations.

Breaking Down the Walls

Unity doesn't mean we all have to agree on everything. But it does mean we have to:

- Share **core values** (like professionalism, education, client safety, and fair regulation).

- Recognize **mutual interests** across specialties.

- Support **industry-wide advocacy**, even when it doesn't directly affect us.

For example, when massage therapists face changes in licensure, it's not "their problem"—it's *our* industry's problem. What affects one segment today may affect another tomorrow.

Ways to Foster Professional Unity

1. **Support multi-specialty associations** that promote broad industry health.

2. **Host local or virtual mixers** that bring different specialties together to share updates, strategies, and resources.

3. **Invite speakers from other beauty disciplines** to your events or classrooms.

4. **Cross-promote advocacy efforts** across beauty categories.

5. **Create mentorship opportunities** that bridge gaps between professionals in different stages and specialties.

Unity is Not Optional—It's Survival

We must begin to think collectively, move collectively, and rise collectively. Our futures are intertwined. The sooner we recognize that, the stronger our position becomes in protecting our licenses, shaping policies, and ensuring that our profession is not treated as disposable.

Action Steps:

*   Identify one way you can **collaborate with a professional outside your specialty** this month.

*   Host or attend a local **"Beauty & Barber Unity" event** or virtual town hall.

*   Follow and support at least one **multi-disciplinary organization or advocacy group**.

*   Start a **roundtable conversation** in your salon, school, or professional group about what unity means in real terms.

Chapter 11
Do You Know What's Happening in Your State?

"When you stay ready, you don't have to get ready."
– A reminder for every licensed professional

There's a reason this chapter shares the title of the book. It's the heartbeat of this message, the pulse of what professionals in cosmetology, barbering, aesthetics, massage therapy, and nail care are facing today.

Across the country, there is a legislative shift happening—some slow and subtle, others sudden and seismic. These shifts are challenging the very foundation of licensure, regulation, and accountability in the beauty and wellness professions.

Understanding the Role of State Agencies

Every licensed professional is governed by a state regulatory agency. This agency may go by different names depending on your state: it might be a Board of Cosmetology and Barbering, a Department of Licensing, a Commission, or even a combined occupational board.

These agencies are tasked with:

- Granting and renewing licenses

- Conducting inspections

- Holding disciplinary hearings

- Approving school curriculums

- Ensuring public safety and professional standards

But here's what most professionals don't realize: these agencies don't exist forever. Many operate under what's called a **"sunset clause."**

What Is a Sunset Clause?

A sunset clause is a legal expiration date for a government agency or program. Unless the legislature actively votes to **renew or extend** the agency, it dissolves on the sunset date. This is intended as a check-and-balance process—but in some states, it's being used as a **back door to deregulation.**

That means your agency, your license, and your career could be at risk not because of a vote against you—but because of inaction, language loopholes, or a lack of public awareness.

⚠ Legislative Update: Oklahoma's HB 1030 and SB 676

Oklahoma has become one of the most closely watched states in the country regarding this issue. Here's what's been unfolding:

- **HB 1030** was introduced in an attempt to extend the life of the Oklahoma State Board of Cosmetology and Barbering. But the bill **lacked clear language** to **transfer the agency** under a new jurisdiction.

Without this supportive language, the bill failed—putting the entire industry at risk of deregulation.

- The defeat of HB 1030 meant that Oklahoma was **on track to become the first state in the nation to fully deregulate** cosmetology and barbering—an outcome with national implications.

- As the session progressed, a new piece of legislation emerged: **SB 676**, introduced as a **Conference Committee Substitute**.

- SB 676 successfully passed and **granted the agency a one-year extension**, temporarily avoiding deregulation.

However, **this is not a final solution**. The bill only delays the sunset date. Unless a permanent jurisdictional transfer or supportive legislation is passed in the next year, the risk of deregulation remains very real.

Why this matters to every state: If it can happen in one, it can happen in others. The playbook is being written in real time. This is why being aware and engaged is no longer optional—it's essential.

What You Can Do Right Now

1. **Visit Your State's Legislative Website**
   Learn how to track bills, committee hearings, and vote records. Every state has its own portal, and many allow you to create alerts for keywords or bill numbers.

2. **Look Up Your Licensing Agency**
   Find out when your board or agency is up for review or sunset. Mark your calendar with any renewal cycles or legislative deadlines that affect you.

3. **Know the Signs of Legislative Change**
   Watch for terms like:

- "Sunset Review"

- "Occupational Licensing Reform"

- "Transfer of Authority"

- "Substitute Bill" or "Omnibus Bill"

4. **Build Relationships With Lawmakers**
   Don't wait until your license is under threat to start making calls or writing letters. Advocacy works best when it starts early and comes from a place of education, not just emotion.

National Implications

Oklahoma is not an outlier—it's a **signal**. Deregulation efforts are being introduced in various forms across the U.S., often quietly. Some are embedded in larger bills. Some target only one profession at a time. Others come under the banner of "reducing red tape" or "expanding economic opportunity."

Action Steps

- Find your state's legislative calendar

- Identify your state representative and senator

- Ask your agency when the next review or sunset is scheduled

- Join a professional organization that tracks legislative threats (see Chapter 12 and Appendix D)

- Educate your clients and colleagues on what's happening

Remember: If you don't know what's happening in your state, by the time you find out—it may already be too late to act.

Chapter 12
Building a Culture of Ongoing Engagement

Legislation, regulations, and professional standards are not static—they evolve. That's why building a culture of engagement isn't just a one-time response to a single bill; it's a mindset and movement that needs to be embedded into the very fabric of our industry.

Too often, beauty professionals only become involved when their livelihood is directly threatened. While that reactive energy is powerful, imagine how much stronger our voice would be if we remained proactive year-round.

Turning Crisis Into Commitment

In every chapter leading up to this one, we've explored how regulation, governance, and advocacy intersect with our work behind the chair or in the treatment room. But here's a hard truth: if we want to protect our licenses, define our own standards, and shape the future of our profession, we must stay engaged beyond the "emergency phase."

The only way to do that is to **build habits, create support systems, and nurture leadership within the industry.**

What Ongoing Engagement Looks Like

Ongoing engagement doesn't require you to be politically active every day, but it does require awareness and participation in key areas:

- **Stay Educated Year-Round**
  Regularly visit your state's cosmetology board website. Sign up for alerts, follow them on social media, and review any changes to rules or pending legislation. Set a reminder to check in once a month.

- **Support and Build Professional Associations**
  If you're not already part of a professional group—local or national—consider joining one. If your area doesn't have one, you can create a simple local chapter or discussion circle. Community keeps momentum alive.

- **Make Advocacy Part of Continuing Education**
  Encourage schools, salons, and independent educators to include industry legislation in their training programs. A strong foundation of knowledge prepares future professionals to lead.

- **Mentorship for Advocacy**
  Identify up-and-coming leaders in your salon or community who have passion and integrity. Mentorship is how we pass down both skill and strategy.

- **Normalize Political Awareness in the Industry**
  Talk about these issues in casual conversations. Share a post, bring it up during professional meetups, or wear a T-shirt that starts a conversation. Awareness is contagious.

The Ripple Effect of Culture Shift

When we build a culture where it's normal to care, to ask questions, and to show up, we begin to redefine what it means to be a beauty professional. No longer just practitioners of a craft—we become stakeholders in a legacy.

Your engagement can inspire someone else to speak up, show up, or learn something new. That ripple of awareness can reach classrooms, salons, board meetings, and legislative offices.

Action Steps: Keep the Movement Alive

- **Start a Monthly "Legislation Check-In"** with your salon team, classmates, or local professionals.

- **Volunteer** with a professional association or advocacy group—even one hour a month helps.

- **Create a Contact List** of peers who want to stay informed or take part in future advocacy efforts.

- **Use Your Social Media** to educate—not just entertain. Even one post a month can reach someone who didn't know they needed to be involved.

You're More Than a License Holder

You're a change-maker. A culture shifter. A protector of professional excellence. The more we normalize advocacy, the less we'll have to scramble in moments of panic.

The future of our industry won't just be decided in legislative halls. It will be decided in the everyday conversations, the classroom lessons, the mentorship moments, and the willingness of people like you to stay informed and engaged—long after the headlines fade.

Chapter 13
Where Do We Go from Here?

The journey through this book has not only been about understanding the history and current state of our industry's regulation—it's been about waking up. Whether you're a licensed cosmetologist, barber, aesthetician, nail technician, massage therapist, student, educator, or simply someone who cares about professionalism in beauty and wellness, we are all now staring at a moment that demands action.

We've seen how many professionals are unaware, uninformed, or disheartened. But now that you've read this far, you are not among them. You are now part of the informed few who must act—not just for yourself, but for your community and the next generation of beauty professionals.

Let's Reclaim Our Narrative

The government may decide what is legal or illegal. But we decide what is **valuable**.

If regulation collapses, our professional standards do not have to. We can still uphold excellence through **certification**, **training**, and **community accountability**. We can create systems of **peer mentorship**, **mobile education**, and **coalitions** that allow us to thrive in spite of uncertainty.

Special Section: If Deregulation Happens

Whether you picked up this book in the midst of a legislative crisis or found it while searching for guidance, know this: **You are not alone. You are not powerless. You are not invisible.**

Let this book be your guide, your resource, and your call to action. We are stronger when we are informed, unified, and engaged. Your voice matters. Your license matters. You matter.

Let's keep showing up, speaking up, and standing up — together.

Seven Key Points for Navigating a Deregulated Landscape

1. **Don't Panic — Get Informed.**
   Knowledge is power. If deregulation occurs, immediately research the final ruling or law that was passed (or allowed to expire) and find out what exactly has changed. Seek credible sources: the state board's official website, legislative archives, and advocacy groups.

2. **Protect Your Standards and Ethics.**
   Just because a license is no longer legally required doesn't mean your personal and professional standards have to drop. Maintain everything you know to be right: sanitation practices, ethical service delivery, and quality client care.

3. **Create or Align with a Certification Body.**
   A license may no longer be mandated by the state, but certification still holds weight. Begin working with professional organizations or coalitions to create certification programs that verify expertise, hours, and continuing education.

4. **Inform Your Clients and Educate the Public.**
   Clients may not understand what deregulation means. Educate them kindly and clearly. Let them know you are

continuing your education and following high safety protocols. Transparency will build trust.

5. **Collaborate Instead of Compete.**
This is the time for unity. Organize meetings with fellow professionals in your area. Form regional alliances or collectives. Share resources, create referral systems, and brainstorm ways to maintain professional visibility.

6. **Stay in Communication with Policy Makers.**
Even if deregulation happens, the door is never fully closed. Stay vocal. Share your experiences. Be part of roundtables, hearings, and town halls. Push for the establishment of new frameworks that prioritize public safety and industry integrity.

7. **Rebrand Your Role in the Marketplace.**
If the professional titles governed by licensure disappear, you may need to reposition your brand. Terms like "beauty practitioner," "wellness artist," or "independent care specialist" may become more common. But your *expertise* will still set you apart — not the title alone.

Example of the 7 Key Points in a 30/60/90 day of the Post-Deregulation Plan

First 30 Days – *Stabilize & Strategize*

- **1. Confirm the Legislative Changes**
  - Read the official ruling, statute, or bill that passed.

  - Identify how it affects your scope of practice, business operation, and title use.

- **2. Secure Business Legitimacy**
  - Ensure your business is still legally registered with

the state (EIN, DBA, LLC, etc.).

- ○ Renew or update your liability insurance and check coverage without a license.

- **3. Notify Clients Professionally**
  - ○ Create a public-facing statement explaining the changes.

  - ○ Reassure clients of your continued training, sanitation, and service excellence.

- **4. Connect with Advocacy Groups**
  - ○ Join groups like Concerned Beauty & Barber Professionals (www.thecbbp.org) or other associations listed in the resource section.

  - ○ Attend webinars or emergency meetings about your rights and responsibilities.

Days 31–60 – *Rebuild & Reposition*
- **1. Obtain Voluntary Certification**
  - ○ Explore certification options through industry associations.

  - ○ If no certifications exist yet, help create one with a coalition of professionals.

- **2. Create a New Professional Bio**
  - ○ Adjust your branding language: "Formerly licensed [title] with X years of experience."

  - ○ Emphasize ongoing education, specialty training, and client results.

- **3. Audit Sanitation & Safety Protocols**
  - Conduct a review of your sanitation processes to align with CDC or professional standards.

  - Document your protocols for client visibility — professionalism still matters.

- **4. Build or Strengthen a Peer Network**
  - Host or attend roundtable discussions with other practitioners in your area.

  - Share referrals, legal updates, client communication tips, and collaborative ideas.

Days 61–90 – *Thrive & Advocate*
- **1. Launch or Join a Local Standardization Movement**
  - Work with peers to create a "Code of Ethics" or "Standards of Practice" for your region.

  - Consider forming a regional advisory council or certification board.

- **2. Communicate with Legislators**
  - Share your experience post-deregulation: what's working, what's harmful, and what you need.

  - Advocate for revised legislation that protects clients and supports professionals.

- **3. Create New Educational Resources**
  - If you're an educator, mentor, or business owner — begin crafting trainings or resources to support others in navigating this shift.

- **4. Document & Reflect**

- ○ Journal your process — what helped, what didn't, and what you learned.

- ○ Consider turning your experience into testimony, articles, or future advocacy work.

Why This Matters for the Nation

What happens in Oklahoma will be watched by the rest of the country. If deregulation occurs here, it could inspire similar efforts elsewhere. This is bigger than any one professional. It's a national call to action. Whether you are in Oklahoma or beyond, the time to act is now — not when the structure collapses, but while we still have power to shape what comes next.

Even without regulation, we can still choose excellence. We can still lead.

Let this be the chapter where the professionals rise — not because we were required to, but because we were committed to.

Acknowledgments

This book would not have been possible without the courage, resilience, and collective spirit of the beauty and barbering community in Oklahoma and beyond.

To the professionals who stood in long meetings, who wrote letters, who stayed after hours researching bills, and who refused to be silent when it would have been easier to look away — thank you. Your determination fueled these pages.

To the individuals and organizations who kept us informed and organized—especially The Concerned Beauty and Barber Professionals, independent educators, and policy watchdogs — your commitment to preserving the integrity of our industry has not gone unnoticed.

To the clients who support us not only with their dollars, but with their advocacy, their listening ears, and their social media shares — you are part of this movement too.

To my fellow authors, mentors, and industry peers: thank you for your encouragement, your wisdom, and your trust.

And to my family and loved ones, especially those who gave me space and grace during the long hours of research and writing — I am deeply grateful.

This book is not just my story—it's ours.

Together, we're writing history.

Appendix A Understanding the Legislative Process & Session Timelines

What Is a Legislative Session?

A legislative session is the official period when your state's lawmakers meet to propose, debate, and pass laws that can directly impact your profession and livelihood.

- In **Oklahoma**, for example, the session begins on the **first Monday in February** and ends by the **last Friday in May**.

- Many states follow a **biennial (two-year)** legislative cycle. This means bills introduced in an **odd-numbered year** (like 2025) can be carried into the next year (2026). If not passed by the end of the second year, the bill **dies** and must be refiled.

Key Legislative Terms to Know

Term	Definition
Bill	A proposed law that must go through several steps to become official.
Committee	A group of legislators who review and edit the bill before it moves forward.
Chamber	Each state has two chambers (House and Senate) that must both approve a bill.
Veto	When the governor rejects a bill.
Override	When the legislature votes to pass the bill despite a veto.
Carryover Bill	A bill that can be considered in the second year of the session without refiling.
Dead Bill	A bill that didn't pass and will not continue—must restart in a future session.
Special Session	A legislative session called outside the regular schedule for urgent issues.

Step-by-Step: How a Bill Becomes a Law

1. **Pre-Filing**
   Legislators file bills ahead of the session.

2. **Introduction**
   The bill is formally introduced in either the House or Senate.

3. **Committee Review**
   The bill is assigned to a committee that can amend, approve, or reject it.

4. **Chamber Vote**
   If approved by the committee, the bill goes to the full chamber for debate and vote.

5. **Second Chamber**
   If passed, it goes to the opposite chamber to repeat the process.

6. **Governor's Desk**
   If both chambers approve, it goes to the governor to sign, veto, or let it pass without a signature.

How to Track a Bill in Your State

- Visit your state legislature's official website. (Example: www. oklegislature.gov for Oklahoma)

- Look for a **"Bill Search"** or **"Legislation Tracker"** feature.

- Use the bill number or keywords (e.g., "cosmetology license") to search.

- Check the **bill summary, status, votes,** and **amendments.**

Pro Tip for Beauty and Barber Professionals

Be proactive—not reactive.
Don't wait until a law is passed to find out how it affects your profession. Tracking bills early gives you time to rally support, testify, or request changes.

- Join advocacy groups like **The Concerned Beauty and Barber Professionals** (www.thecbbp.org) or your state's local associations.

- Stay in contact with legislators, especially those on professional regulation committees.

Bonus Timeline: What to Do in the First 30/60/90 Days After a New Law Is Passed

Timeframe	Action
First 30 Days	Read the full bill and highlight what applies to your license or business. Share with peers.
Day 31–60	Join webinars, attend state board updates, or ask your association how this changes compliance.
Day 61–90	Adjust your business, update services or signage, and educate your team or clients as needed.

Bill Tracker Worksheet

Date	Bill Number	Title of Bill	Action Taken	Notes

(Make several printable copies or create a digital version you can update as you go.)

Final Note

Whether you're a **cosmetologist, barber, nail technician, aesthetician, natural hair stylist, braider, massage therapist,** or part of any beauty profession, knowing how your legislative session works **equips you to show up, speak up, and stand up** when it matters most.

Appendix B Advocacy, Professional, and Legislative Resources

This appendix serves as your go-to directory for staying connected, engaged, and informed. Whether you're writing a letter to your legislator, joining a professional association, or attending your first legislative

Professional Associations and Advocacy Groups

These organizations provide support, education, and advocacy specific to beauty and wellness professionals:

Organization	Website	Focus
The Concerned Beauty and Barber Professionals (CBBP)	thecbbp.org	Advocacy, education, and representation for beauty and barber professionals.
Professional Beauty Association (PBA)	probeauty.org	National organization advocating for cosmetology and barbering careers.
Beauty Changes Lives	beautychangeslives.org	Scholarships, mentorship, and industry elevation.
Associated Hair Professionals (AHP)	associatedhairprofessionals.com	Resources, liability insurance, and career support.
Associated Skin Care Professionals (ASCP)	ascpskincare.com	For estheticians and skin care professionals—insurance, education, and support.
Associated Nail Professionals (ANP)	nailprofessionals.com	Advocacy and liability coverage for nail techs.
National Coalition of Estheticians, Manufacturers/Distributors & Associations (NCEA)	ncea.tv	Focused on continuing education and advanced credentialing.

State Board and Legislative Resources

These tools help you stay informed about laws, licensing, and proposed legislation in your state.

Resource	Description
Oklahoma State Board of Cosmetology and Barbering	ok.gov/cosmo – Licensing, board meetings, regulations, and public notices.
Oklahoma Legislature	oklegislature.gov – Bill tracking, legislative calendars, and contact info for representatives and senators.
National Conference of State Legislatures (NCSL)	ncsl.org – Nonpartisan resource on policy, licensing trends, and national legislation.
OpenStates.org	openstates.org – Search and track legislation across the U.S.

Advocacy + Leadership Tools

Whether you're writing a letter or preparing to testify, these resources can help.

- **Bill Tracker Worksheet**
  Use this to record a bill number, track its progress, and note dates and sponsors. *(A sample is included in Appendix C)*

- **Email + Phone Scripts**
  Pre-written language for reaching out to legislators. *(Also found in Appendix C)*

- **Social Media Templates**
  Graphics and sample posts for raising awareness online.

- **Public Testimony Guide**
  Tips and structure for delivering a strong, respectful message during legislative hearings.

Mental Fitness Resources for Advocates

Advocacy can be emotionally draining. Here's how to protect your peace while staying committed.

Resource	Use
Mentally Fit Behind the Chair Book and Journal	Support your emotional well-being while advocating for your industry.
Calm App / Insight Timer / Headspace	Guided meditations to relieve anxiety before public speaking or political meetings.
Therapy or Group Coaching	Consider regular support during high-stress legislative seasons.

Appendix C Templates & Scripts

This appendix is designed to make advocacy easier by giving you tools you can copy, customize, and confidently use. Whether you're contacting your legislator, tracking a bill, or preparing to speak at a hearing—this section is your toolkit.

Sample Email to a Legislator

Subject Line: Support for [Bill Name or Number] – From a Concerned Beauty & Barber Professional.

Body:

Dear [Representative/Senator Last Name],

My name is [Your Full Name], and I am a licensed [cosmetologist/ barber/nail technician/aesthetician/massage therapist] in [City, State]. I am writing to express my [support/opposition] to [Bill Number or Name], currently being considered in the [House/Senate].

This bill directly impacts our industry, which includes thousands of small business owners and licensed professionals across the state. [Insert a personal story, fact, or statistic about how the bill would affect you, your clients, or your livelihood.]

I respectfully ask that you [vote in favor of / oppose] this legislation and consider the voices of those of us who serve our communities daily.

Thank you for your time and service.

Sincerely,
[Your Full Name]
[Your License Type & Number, if applicable]
[Your City, State]
[Phone Number or Email Address]

Phone Call Script for Legislators

"Hello, my name is [Your Name], and I'm a licensed [profession] in [City/State]. I'm calling to express my [support/opposition] to [Bill Number or Title].

This bill directly affects my livelihood and the clients I serve.

Please let [Senator/Representative Name] know that I'd like them to [vote for/against] this bill.

Thank you for your time."

Public Comment/Testimony Template

If you are speaking at a hearing or public meeting, use this outline:

Introduction:

- "Good morning/afternoon. My name is [Your Name]. I am a licensed [profession] and a resident of [City, State]."

Personal Impact:

- "I have been working in this industry for [X] years and have served hundreds of clients. This bill would [briefly explain the impact—positive or negative]."

Broader Concern:

- "This legislation affects not just me, but thousands of professionals across the state. Many of us are small business owners who contribute to the economy and serve vulnerable populations."

Call to Action:

- "I urge you to [support/oppose] this bill and take into consideration the voices of those working daily in the field."

Closing:

- "Thank you for the opportunity to speak. I am happy to answer any questions."

Client Testimonial Request Template

Purpose: Empower clients to share how beauty/barber professionals impact their lives. These testimonials can be included in letters to legislators, websites, or used during public comment periods.

Email/Text Message/Printed Template:

Subject: Share Your Voice – Help Support Licensed Beauty & Barber Professionals

Dear [Client Name],

As a licensed [cosmetologist/barber/nail tech/aesthetician/massage therapist], I take great pride in the service I provide to you and others in our community. Right now, legislation is being proposed that could impact how we practice and protect our licenses.

Your voice matters too. Would you be willing to write a short statement about how the services you receive have positively impacted your life?

You can use the guide below to help:

- Your name (or initials if you'd like to remain anonymous)

- How long you've been a client

- How services like haircare, skincare, or massage have helped you (health, mental wellness, self-esteem, convenience, trust in licensed care, etc.)

- Why professional licensing and sanitation standards matter to you

Example Testimonial:
"I've been going to [Pro Name] for 5 years. As someone with alopecia, the care I receive has made a huge difference in my confidence and overall well-being. I trust licensed professionals because they are trained, knowledgeable, and consistent. I wouldn't want just anyone touching my scalp or skin."

Thank you for standing with us,
[Your Name]

Client Letter to Legislators

Subject: Please Support Licensed Beauty Professionals

Dear [Legislator's Name],

My name is [Your Name], and I am a client and supporter of licensed beauty professionals in our community. I am writing today because I'm deeply concerned about proposed legislation that could deregulate the cosmetology and barbering industry in our state.

The professionals who care for our hair, skin, and nails are trained, licensed, and committed to providing safe services. I personally rely on these services not just for appearance, but for overall hygiene, confidence, and well-being.

Removing licensure puts public health at risk and undermines an industry that is a vital part of our community and economy. I ask that you please protect licensure standards and support those who serve us with skill, care, and professionalism.

Thank you for your time and service.

Sincerely,
[Your Name]
[City, State]

School or Salon Owner Letter to Legislators

Subject: Protect Our Licensed Beauty Professionals and the Future of Our Industry

Dear [Legislator's Name],

I am [Your Name], the owner of [School/Salon Name] in [City/State]. I am writing with deep concern regarding proposed legislation that would deregulate the cosmetology and barbering industry in our state.

As a business owner who trains and employs licensed professionals, I have seen firsthand the importance of education, sanitation, and technical skill in our field. Removing licensure requirements would lower professional standards, endanger public health, and dismantle a pathway to entrepreneurship for thousands.

Our school/salon plays a critical role in community development and workforce readiness. I ask that you oppose deregulation and instead support legislation that uplifts, rather than dismantles, our profession.

Thank you for your attention to this critical issue.

Respectfully,
[Your Name]
[Title/Owner, School/Salon Name]
[City, State]

Educator or Student Letter to Legislators

Subject: Protect the Future of Cosmetology & Barbering Education

Dear [Legislator's Name],

My name is [Your Name], and I am a [student/instructor] at [School

Name] in [City, State]. I am writing to express my concern about legislation that may deregulate the beauty and barber industry in our state.

I have chosen this profession because it offers a legitimate, licensed career path rooted in education, hygiene, public service, and creativity. My training has included sanitation, anatomy, product chemistry, and client care — all critical to ensuring safety.

Removing licensure would harm our ability to grow, earn, and serve our communities responsibly. Please protect our future by keeping the industry regulated and professionally recognized.

Sincerely,
[Your Name]
[Student/Educator, School Name]
[City, State]

General Public/Supporter Letter to Legislators

Subject: Please Keep Beauty and Barbering Professionals Licensed

Dear [Legislator's Name],

I am writing as a concerned member of the public who values the skill, hygiene, and professionalism of licensed beauty and barbering professionals in our state.

Our barbers, nail techs, estheticians, cosmetologists, and massage therapists go through rigorous training and licensing to provide safe, regulated services to the public. They are small business owners, caregivers, and trusted service providers in our communities.

Please oppose legislation that threatens licensure in this profession. Our health, safety, and economic stability are too important to compromise.

Thank you for considering this important issue.

Sincerely,
[Your Name]
[City, State]

1. Phone Call Script to a Legislator's Office

"Hi, my name is [Your Name], and I'm a licensed [cosmetologist/ barber/nail tech/aesthetician/massage therapist] in your district. I'm calling to ask that you [support/oppose] [Bill Number or Topic], which would impact our profession. This legislation affects how we serve our clients and maintain our livelihoods. I'd appreciate your support and would love to share more of my story if that would be helpful. Thank you for your time."

2. In-Person Talking Point (e.g., Capitol Day or Town Hall)

"Good afternoon. My name is [Your Name], and I've been in the [beauty/barber/wellness] industry for [#] years. I'm here today to ask you to please consider how [Bill Topic] will affect small businesses like mine. We provide more than just haircuts or facials— we help people feel confident, manage health-related concerns, and support our local economy. I'm asking you to please [support/ oppose] [Bill Number]."

3. Student Voice Prompt (for School Visits or Youth Testimony)

"Hello, I'm a student at [School Name] studying to become a licensed [profession]. This career means everything to me because it allows me to express my creativity and help others feel good about themselves. Please don't take away the opportunity for people like me to succeed in this field. We are the future of this industry."

4. Letter or Email Closing Statement Prompt

"Thank you for the work you do in our community. I hope you'll stand with professionals like me and recognize the positive impact we make every day. I'd be honored to speak more about how this legislation affects our profession."

Pro Tips for Advocacy

- **Keep it brief.** Legislators are busy—get to the point quickly.

- **Be respectful.** Passion is powerful, but professionalism makes a lasting impression.

- **Know your bill number.** If you're referencing legislation, include the official number and title if possible.

- **Share a personal story.** Humanizing your message helps make an impact.

- **Follow up.** Thank them for their time and send a quick email if you met in person.

Respect is Power: Speaking with Legislators the Right Way

It's normal to feel frustrated, scared, or angry about legislation that threatens your career. But when you're speaking to legislators — whether by phone, email, or in person — **respect is non-negotiable**.

Why It Matters:

- **Legislators are people** — and like anyone else, they respond better when approached with calm professionalism.

- Even if they *disagree*, your respectful tone can **keep the door open** for future conversations.

- Advocacy is about building relationships, not just winning arguments.

How to Stay Respectful and Clear:

- Speak with **gratitude** for their time and service.

- Use **"I" statements** to express how a bill impacts you.

- Stick to the **facts**, not assumptions or attacks.

- If you're emotional, breathe and **pause before responding**.

- Say thank you — even if you don't get the response you hoped for.

Appendix D Additional Resources

For Continued Learning, Connection, and Advocacy

National Professional Organizations

- **Professional Beauty Association (PBA)** – probeauty.org
  Offers resources, networking opportunities, legislative advocacy, and professional development tools for beauty professionals.

- **American Association of Cosmetology Schools (AACS)** – beautyschools.org
  Provides advocacy, professional development, and school support in cosmetology education.

- **The Concerned Beauty and Barber Professionals (TheCBBP) / Politics Beauty/Barber (PBB)** thecbbp.org
  Continuing education in health and safety for Beauty and Barber Professionals and advocacy state-to-state to strengthen the profession and the professional license.

State Boards & Government Resources

- **Oklahoma State Board of Cosmetology and Barbering** – oklahoma.gov/cosmo

- **Oklahoma Legislature Bill Search and Tracking** – www. oklegislature.gov
  (Use these links as examples—customize based on your state for local editions.)

Educational and Legislative Advocacy Platforms

- **Ballot Ready** – ballotready.org
  Offers personalized election ballots and information about

local officials and candidates.

- **Common Cause** – commoncause.org
  A platform for empowering civic participation and tracking policy reforms.

- **OpenStates.org** – openstates.org
  Allows you to follow legislation, learn about lawmakers, and track bills by state.

Books & Publications

- *Mentally Fit Behind the Chair* by Asrar Johnson
  A guide to wellness and mindset for beauty professionals.

- *SalonSational* by Asrar Johnson
  Professional development strategies for those in cosmetology and barbering.

- **Recommended Reading for Advocates**:

  - *Advocacy for Beginners* by Shawn Burns

  - *The Beauty Industry Survival Guide* by Tina Alberino

Podcasts & Media

- *Shear Madness Podcast* – Covers business, mental health, and the beauty industry.

- *Hair Love Radio* – Personal development for stylists and entrepreneurs.

Continuing Education Platforms

- **Milady Training** – miladytraining.com

- **Beauty Cast Network** – beautycastnetwork.com

Appendix E
Professional Development & Leadership Pathways in the Beauty and Barbering Industry

This appendix is designed to inspire and inform beauty and barber professionals about the many ways they can continue growing—beyond the chair and into leadership, education, advocacy, and entrepreneurship. Whether you're new to the field or a seasoned professional, there is always another level.

1. Educational & Industry Advancement

- **Become an Educator**:
  Consider teaching at a beauty school or becoming a continuing education provider. You'll not only shape the next generation, but gain a deeper understanding of your craft.

- **Pursue Instructor Licensure**:
  Many states require specific coursework and testing. Check your state board's requirements.

- **Attend Conferences & Expos**:
  Stay current with trends, laws, and innovation. Events like Bronner Bros, Premiere, ISSE, and others are great networking opportunities.

- **Advanced Certifications**:
  Explore niche certifications in areas such as:
  - Trichology/Dermotricology
  - Esthetics and Advanced Esthetics
  - Lash Artistry and PMU
  - Natural Hair Care & Braiding

- ○   Oncology Aesthetics

- ○   Product Formulation

2. Business & Entrepreneurial Growth

- **Open or Expand a Business**:
  Whether a solo suite, full salon, or wellness center, this is a path to ownership and creative freedom.

- **Develop a Product Line**:
  Create your own hair, skin, or wellness products that reflect your expertise and values.

- **Write a Book or Create a Course**:
  Share your journey, systems, or success tips with others in the industry.

- **Start a Podcast or YouTube Channel**:
  Use your voice and story to inspire others. You can educate and entertain while building your brand.

3. Advocacy & Industry Leadership

- **Join a Board or Committee**:
  Get involved with your state's regulatory board, advisory panels, or national associations.

- **Policy Advocate**:
  Attend legislative sessions, write letters, and connect with lawmakers to protect and progress the industry.

- **Mentorship Programs**:
  Support emerging professionals and help bridge gaps in skills, ethics, and leadership.

4. Collaboration & Community Leadership

- **Create or Join a Collective**:
  Collaborate with like-minded professionals for events, education, or community service.

- **Host Events or Educational Seminars**:
  Become the go-to expert in your community by offering public or industry-specific sessions.

- **Speak at Schools or Conferences**:
  Inspire students and professionals with your journey, expertise, and lessons learned.

5. Professional Associations to Consider Joining

- Professional Beauty Association (PBA)

- American Association of Cosmetology Schools (AACS)

- International Association of Trichologists (IAT)

- Associated Skin Care Professionals (ASCP)

- National Barber Museum and Hall of Fame

- State-specific boards and unions

- The concern beauty barber professionals (CBBP)

Final Encouragement:
You are more than a service provider — you are a visionary, an advocate, and a leader. Your career doesn't have to stop at the chair. Keep evolving, learning, and showing up for yourself and your community.

Appendix F
Glossary of Terms

This glossary is designed to help readers, especially those new to legislation or advocacy work, better understand the terminology commonly used in discussions about lawmaking, state boards, and professional regulation. These terms can help you confidently engage in conversations, write letters, and participate in meetings or hearings.

A

- **Advocacy**: The act of supporting or arguing for a cause, policy, or group—such as speaking up for beauty industry professionals during legislative sessions.

- **Amendment**: A formal change or addition proposed to a bill or law.

- **Appropriations Bill**: A type of legislation that allows government spending. Not all bills deal with money, but those that do often require a separate appropriations bill.

B

- **Bill**: A draft version of a proposed law presented for approval to a legislative body.

- **Bill Author**: The lawmaker who introduces the bill and advocates for its passage.

- **Bill Number**: A unique identifying number given to a bill once introduced (e.g., HB123 or SB456).

- **Biennial Legislation**: In some states, the legislature meets every two years (biennially), or considers certain bills in a two-year cycle. If a bill is introduced in an odd-numbered year and is not passed or voted down, it may be "carried over" and reconsidered during the even-numbered year of the same session—unless it is declared dead.

C

- **Committee**: A group of legislators assigned to review bills in detail before sending them to the full chamber for a vote.

- **Cosmetology Board**: A state agency responsible for licensing, regulating, and overseeing professionals in the beauty and barbering industries. May include estheticians, nail techs, barbers, and other specialty fields.

D

- **Debate**: A formal discussion where lawmakers express their support or opposition to a bill.

- **Deregulation**: The process of removing government regulations—in this context, removing license requirements for certain professions.

E

- **Effective Date**: The date when a new law or amendment officially goes into effect.

- **Executive Director**: The head of a state board or agency, often responsible for implementing policies and overseeing operations.

F

- **Floor Vote**: The final vote taken by a full legislative chamber (House or Senate) after debate and amendments.

H

- **Hearing**: A formal meeting where testimony is given for or against a bill, often including public comment.

- **House**: One of the two chambers in most state legislatures (the other is the Senate).

L

- **Licensure**: A legal requirement to obtain and maintain a license in order to practice a profession.

- **Lobbyist**: A person hired to influence lawmakers on behalf of a specific interest group or organization.

P

- **Public Comment**: The portion of a hearing or process where members of the public can share opinions, either written or verbal, on a bill.

- **Profession in Transition**: A term sometimes used to describe beauty specialties undergoing changes in regulation (e.g., braiding, lashes, natural haircare).

R

- **Regulation**: Rules established by a governing body that control how a profession operates.

- **Representative**: A lawmaker who serves in the House chamber at the state level.

- **Resolution**: A formal statement adopted by a legislative body that may express opinion or intent but does not carry the force of law.

S

- **Senator**: A lawmaker who serves in the Senate chamber at the state level.

- **Session**: The official period when a legislative body meets to discuss and vote on proposed bills. Most states have annual sessions; some are biennial.

- **Statute**: A written law passed by a legislative body.

T

- **Testimony**: A statement given during a public hearing to provide facts, opinions, or support/opposition to a bill.

Appendix G Continuing Your Advocacy Journey

Advocacy is not a one-time event—it's a continuous process. Whether you've made your first call to a legislator or stood at the Capitol with fellow professionals, your voice matters every step of the way. This appendix is here to guide you as you move from one season of advocacy to the next.

Sustaining Momentum: What to Do After the Legislative Session Ends

- **Debrief and Reflect**
  - What went well? What did you learn?

  - Take notes on your experience to improve your strategy for next time.

- **Celebrate Your Wins**
  - A bill doesn't have to pass to be a victory. Awareness, increased engagement, and media coverage are big wins.

- **Reconnect With Your Network**
  - Thank those who showed up with you—whether physically or virtually.

  - Stay in touch with organizations and coalitions that supported your efforts.

- **Continue Building Relationships**
  - Send a thank-you note or email to your legislator—even if they didn't vote your way. Respect builds bridges.

Everyday Advocacy: Simple, Consistent Actions You Can Take

- **Stay Informed**
  - Subscribe to your state legislature's newsletter or alert system.

  - Follow your local board or licensing agency on social media.

- **Share and Educate**
  - Post educational content on social media to inform clients and peers.

  - Host short info sessions or town halls at your salon, school, or via Zoom.

- **Support Advocacy Groups**
  - Join coalitions or task forces.

  - Volunteer your space for meetings or education nights.

- **Stay Visible**
  - Write letters to the editor in local newspapers.

  - Speak up at town halls or agency meetings—even when there's no immediate bill on the table.

Strategic Growth: Leveling Up Your Advocacy
- **Mentor Someone New**
  - Help another professional get involved. Share this book, walk them through the legislative process, or take them with you to a Capitol Day.

- **Get Involved in Leadership**
  - Join advisory boards, school curriculum committees,

or apply to serve on your state's regulatory board when positions open up.

- **Pursue Continued Education in Policy**
  - Take free or low-cost classes about state government, public speaking, or nonprofit advocacy.

- **Partner With Other Industries**
  - Connect with nursing, education, and labor unions who are also fighting for professional protections and fair legislation.

Your Journey, Your Legacy

Change doesn't always happen in one session or one year—but every action creates ripples. You're not only shaping your future, but paving the way for students, apprentices, and even the next generation of advocates. Let this appendix serve as your reminder. *You don't need to be a politician to make political impact—you just need to care enough to act.*

Appendix H Sample Advocacy Journal Pages

Whether you're attending your first Capitol Day, calling a legislator, or simply observing how a bill moves through your statehouse, journaling your advocacy experiences can keep you organized, encouraged, and clear on your long-term goals. Below are sample pages that readers can print or recreate in their own journals, advocacy binders, or digital notebooks.

Advocacy Journal Page Template 1: Legislative Interaction Log

Date of Contact:
Legislator/Office Contacted:
Contact Method: (phone, email, in person, social media, letter)
Issue/Bill Discussed:
Key Talking Points You Shared:

- **Response Received (if any):**
- **Follow-Up Action Needed:**
  [ ] Send thank you
  [ ] Email more info
  [ ] Schedule follow-up
  [ ] Invite to visit salon/school
  [ ] Other: _____

Advocacy Journal Page Template 2: Capitol Day Notes

Date of Capitol Visit:
Purpose of Visit/Key Bill(s):
Who Attended With You:
Meetings Attended:

- **Key Highlights:**
- **Challenges or Surprises:**

- **Next Steps to Take:**
- **Personal Reflection:**
  How did this experience make you feel? What would you do differently next time?

Advocacy Journal Page Template 3: Year-in-Review

Year:
Bills I Tracked:

- **Advocacy Activities I Participated In:**
  [ ] Called a legislator
  [ ] Attended a Capitol Day
  [ ] Hosted an info session
  [ ] Wrote a letter/email
  [ ] Met with a policymaker
  [ ] Posted about legislation online
  [ ] Joined a coalition/group
  [ ] Other: _____

Biggest Wins This Year:

- **Lessons Learned:**
- **My Advocacy Goal for Next Year:**

These pages are meant to be flexible and personal. They help you look back at your growth as an advocate, stay accountable to your mission, and inspire others by example.

Notes & Reflections

Use this space to jot down any final thoughts, breakthroughs, action steps, or personal reflections inspired by this guide. Your voice matters, and your next step starts here.

Author's Note

This book was written from the heart of a professional who has stood behind the chair, in the treatment room, in classrooms, on salon floors, and at the State Capitol. I wrote it not just as a practitioner, but as a witness to what happens when our industry is misunderstood, undervalued, or underrepresented in spaces where decisions are made.

In my journey, I've also served as an inspector and examiner for the State Board of Cosmetology and Barbering, which deepened my understanding of the regulatory systems that shape our profession. Today, I continue to advocate for our field as a proud member advocate with the **Concerned Beauty and Barbering Professionals**, representing Oklahoma and working alongside others committed to the advancement and protection of our industry.

My hope is that you—the cosmetologist, barber, aesthetician, nail tech, massage therapist, student, educator, school owner, client, or community supporter—walk away from these pages with a renewed sense of your power. Advocacy doesn't require perfection. It requires presence. It requires the courage to stand, even when your voice shakes.

I don't have all the answers. But I do have experience, and a deep belief that together we can do more than just protect this industry—we can transform it.

Thank you for showing up. For asking questions. For leading with purpose. For choosing to be a part of something bigger than one salon, one classroom, or one bill.

I'll see you on the frontlines.
With purpose and solidarity,

—Asrar Johnson
Dermotricologist, Educator, Advocate
Studio Noir Dermotricology & Wellness

www.ingramcontent.com/pod-product-compliance
Lightning Source LLC
Chambersburg PA
CBHW062043270326
41929CB00014B/2524